Tamagoyaki cookbook 101
Master the Art of Japanese Rolled Omelette with 20 Delicious Recipes

While every precaution has been taken in the preparation of this book, the publisher assumes no responsibility for errors or omissions, or for damages resulting from the use of the information contained herein.

TAMAGOYAKI COOKBOOK 101

First edition. November 6, 2023.

Copyright © 2023 john ahmad.

ISBN: 979-8223502272

Written by john ahmad.

John Ahmad

Chapter Outline:

Chapter 1: Introduction to Tamagoyaki

Tamagoyaki, the artful Japanese rolled omelette, has captivated food enthusiasts for generations with its delicate layers and irresistible flavors. In this chapter, we'll take you on a journey into the world of Tamagoyaki, exploring its cultural significance, essential ingredients, and the techniques required to create this culinary masterpiece.

Originating in Japan, Tamagoyaki holds a special place in the country's culinary heritage. It has been enjoyed for centuries, both as a standalone dish and as a versatile ingredient in various Japanese meals. The cultural context surrounding Tamagoyaki adds depth and appreciation to the art of its creation.

To create a perfect Tamagoyaki, it's crucial to understand the essential ingredients and equipment. The star of the show is, of course, the eggs. Fresh, high-quality eggs make a significant difference in both taste and texture. Other key ingredients include dashi (Japanese stock), soy sauce, mirin (sweet rice wine), and salt. We'll guide you through selecting the right eggs and seasonings to achieve the ideal balance of flavors.

When it comes to equipment, a rectangular Tamagoyaki pan, also known as a makiyakinabe, is essential. Its shape allows for even cooking and rolling of the omelette. Additionally, a pair of chopsticks or a special Tamagoyaki spatula will help you achieve those distinct layers. We'll provide guidance on choosing the right pan and utensils to ensure successful Tamagoyaki-making endeavors.

Now, let's dive into the technique of making Tamagoyaki. The process involves a delicate balance of heat control and precise rolling. We'll walk you through step-by-step instructions, from preparing the egg mixture to rolling the omelette into a beautiful square shape. Along the way, we'll share expert tips to help you master the art of Tamagoyaki with finesse.

While the classic Tamagoyaki recipe is undoubtedly delightful, we'll also introduce you to a world of tantalizing variations. From sweet options with added ingredients like sugar, honey, or sweet soy glaze to savory variations incorporating vegetables, seafood, or even cheese, these adaptations will elevate your Tamagoyaki to new heights. Get ready to explore the exciting possibilities and discover your personal favorites.

As you embark on your Tamagoyaki-making journey, it's essential to be prepared for potential challenges. We'll address common pitfalls and provide troubleshooting tips to help you overcome any obstacles you may encounter along the way. With practice and perseverance, you'll become a Tamagoyaki master in no time.

By the end of this chapter, you'll have a comprehensive understanding of Tamagoyaki, including its cultural significance, essential ingredients, and the fundamental techniques required for successful execution. Now, get ready to equip yourself with the necessary knowledge as we delve into Chapter 2: Essential Equipment and Ingredients, where we'll explore the key tools and components in more detail.

Chapter 2: Essential Equipment and Ingredients

To create authentic and delicious Tamagoyaki, it's essential to have the right equipment and ingredients at your disposal. In this chapter, we'll guide you through selecting the necessary tools and sourcing the finest ingredients to ensure your Tamagoyaki turns out perfectly every time.

Tamagoyaki Pan (Makiyakinabe): The rectangular-shaped Tamagoyaki pan is specifically designed for making rolled omelettes. Its size and shape allow for even heat distribution and easy rolling. Look for a pan with a non-stick surface to prevent the omelette from sticking.

Chopsticks or Tamagoyaki Spatula: These utensils are indispensable for rolling the omelette. Using chopsticks or a Tamagoyaki spatula allows you to lift, fold, and roll the layers with precision. Choose chopsticks or a spatula with a smooth surface to avoid scratching the non-stick coating of the pan.

Whisk or Fork: A whisk or fork is needed to beat the eggs thoroughly. Whisking the eggs ensures a uniform texture and helps incorporate air, resulting in a fluffy and light Tamagoyaki.

Dashi (Japanese Stock): Dashi forms the base of the Tamagoyaki seasoning and adds umami depth to the dish. You can make dashi from scratch using kombu (dried kelp) and bonito flakes, or you can use dashi powder or granules, which are readily available in stores.

Eggs: Fresh and high-quality eggs are crucial for a delicious Tamagoyaki. Seek out eggs from reliable sources, preferably organic or free-range. Using eggs with vibrant yolks will enhance the visual appeal of your rolled omelette.

Soy Sauce: A staple in Japanese cuisine, soy sauce adds a savory note and depth of flavor to Tamagoyaki. Opt for a good-quality soy sauce with a balanced taste, such as a light soy sauce or usukuchi soy sauce.

Mirin (Sweet Rice Wine): Mirin lends a subtle sweetness to Tamagoyaki and helps to caramelize the outer layers, imparting a beautiful glaze. Look for genuine mirin, which is sweet and low in alcohol content, rather than substitutes that may contain high levels of salt or artificial sweeteners.

Salt: A pinch of salt is essential for balancing the flavors in Tamagoyaki. Use a fine-grain salt and add it sparingly, adjusting to your personal taste preferences.

Optional Ingredients: Depending on your desired variation of Tamagoyaki, you may wish to incorporate additional ingredients. These can include thinly sliced scallions, shiitake mushrooms, shrimp, crab, cheese, or any other ingredient that complements your flavor profile.

By having the right equipment and sourcing high-quality ingredients, you'll be well-prepared to create Tamagoyaki with authenticity and finesse. In the next chapter, we'll dive into the technique of making Tamagoyaki, where we'll provide step-by-step instructions to bring your rolled omelette to life. Get ready to roll up your sleeves and embark on a culinary adventure!

Chapter 3: Basic Tamagoyaki Technique

Mastering the basic technique is crucial for creating a perfect Tamagoyaki. In this chapter, we'll guide you through the step-by-step process, sharing detailed instructions, tips, and tricks to help you achieve a beautifully rolled and flavorful omelette every time.

Step 1: Prepare Your Ingredients

Start by gathering your ingredients:

- Eggs: Use fresh, high-quality eggs for the best results. The number of eggs you'll need depends on the desired size of your Tamagoyaki.

- Dashi: If making your own dashi, soak a small piece of kombu (dried kelp) in water overnight and simmer it with katsuobushi (dried bonito flakes) for about 10 minutes. Alternatively, you can use dashi powder or granules dissolved in water.

- Soy Sauce: Opt for a good-quality soy sauce, such as light soy sauce or usukuchi soy sauce, to season your Tamagoyaki.

- Mirin: Genuine mirin, which is sweet and low in alcohol, adds a subtle sweetness and helps caramelize the outer layers of the omelette.

- Salt: A pinch of salt enhances the overall flavor of your Tamagoyaki.

- Optional Ingredients: If desired, prepare optional ingredients like thinly sliced scallions, shiitake mushrooms, shrimp, crab, or cheese to add to your Tamagoyaki.

Step 2: Heat the Tamagoyaki Pan

Place your Tamagoyaki pan over medium heat. Allow it to heat up for a few minutes until it reaches an even temperature. This ensures proper and consistent cooking throughout the process.

Step 3: Season and Cook the First Layer

Lightly oil the pan using a brush or cooking spray to prevent the eggs from sticking. Pour a thin layer of the beaten egg mixture into the pan, tilting the pan gently to evenly spread the egg across the surface. The layer should be thin enough to cook quickly.

Cook the eggs until the edges start to set but the center remains slightly runny. The residual heat will continue to cook the omelette as you roll it later. Be careful not to overcook the first layer, as it should remain moist and soft for easier rolling.

Step 4: Roll the First Layer

Using chopsticks or a Tamagoyaki spatula, gently fold one edge of the cooked egg layer towards the center. Roll it tightly to the opposite side of the pan, ensuring the rolled portion stays intact. Apply gentle pressure with your utensil as you roll to maintain a compact shape and even layers.

Step 5: Make the Second Layer

Add another thin layer of the beaten egg mixture to the exposed part of the pan, ensuring it covers the rolled layer. Tilt the pan once again to distribute the egg evenly. This layer will adhere to the rolled layer, creating a seamless continuation.

Cook the second layer until the edges start to set but the center remains slightly runny. This allows for a smooth transition between layers and ensures the overall texture of the Tamagoyaki remains soft and moist.

Step 6: Roll the Second Layer

Once the second layer has partially cooked, roll the omelette tightly towards the opposite side of the pan, overlapping the first layer. The layers should adhere together smoothly, creating a neat and uniform appearance.

Step 7: Repeat the Process

Continue adding a thin layer of beaten egg mixture, cooking, and rolling until you've used all the egg mixture. Aim for about 4 to 6 layers, depending on your preference and the size of your pan. Each layer should be rolled tightly, ensuring a compact and visually appealing result.

Maintain a consistent heat throughout the process, adjusting it as needed to prevent the layers from overcooking or undercooking.

Step 8: Adjust the Shape

As you roll each layer, use the chopsticks or spatula to gently press the omelette together, ensuring a square shape. Apply slight pressure while rolling to maintain a compact and uniform appearance. This will help create those distinct layers that make Tamagoyaki visually appealing.

Step 9: Remove from the Pan and Cool

Once the Tamagoyaki is fully cooked, carefully transfer it to a cutting board or plate. Allow it to cool slightly before slicing. Cooling helps the layers hold their shape and makes the cutting process easier. The omelette should still be warm when served, so don't let it cool completely.

Step 10: Slice and Serve

Using a sharp knife, slice the Tamagoyaki into bite-sized pieces. Aim for clean, even cuts to showcase the layers within. Arrange the slices beautifully on a serving plate and garnish as desired. Tamagoyaki can be enjoyed warm or at room temperature, making it a versatile and delightful addition to any meal.

With practice, patience, and attention to detail, you'll soon become adept at creating perfectly rolled Tamagoyaki. In the following chapters, we'll explore various delicious Tamagoyaki recipes and innovative variations to expand your culinary repertoire. Get ready to savor the delightful flavors of this iconic Japanese dish!

Chapter 4: Classic Tamagoyaki Recipe

The classic Tamagoyaki recipe is a beloved staple in Japanese cuisine, known for its simplicity and delicious flavors. In this chapter, we'll guide you through the step-by-step process of creating a traditional Tamagoyaki that showcases the delicate layers and savory taste that make this dish so special.

Ingredients:

- 4 large eggs
- 1 tablespoon dashi
- 1 tablespoon soy sauce
- 1 tablespoon mirin
- 1/4 teaspoon salt
- Cooking oil or cooking spray for greasing the pan

Instructions:

1. In a mixing bowl, crack the eggs and beat them until the yolks and whites are well combined. You can use a whisk or a fork for this step.

1. Add dashi, soy sauce, mirin, and salt to the beaten eggs. Whisk the mixture together until all the ingredients are fully incorporated. The dashi and soy sauce add depth of flavor, while the mirin brings a subtle sweetness to the Tamagoyaki.

1. Heat your Tamagoyaki pan over medium heat. Grease the pan with a small amount of cooking oil or use cooking spray to prevent sticking.

1. Pour a thin layer of the egg mixture into the pan, tilting it to ensure even distribution. Cook the eggs until the edges start to

set but the center is still slightly runny. This allows for easier rolling and a moist texture.

1. Using chopsticks or a Tamagoyaki spatula, gently fold one edge of the cooked egg layer towards the center. Roll it tightly to the opposite side of the pan, forming the first layer of the Tamagoyaki. Apply gentle pressure with your utensil as you roll to create a compact and smooth layer.

1. Add another thin layer of the egg mixture to the exposed part of the pan, covering the rolled layer. Tilt the pan to distribute the egg evenly. Cook until the edges start to set but the center remains slightly runny.

1. Roll the omelette tightly once again, overlapping the previous layer. Repeat this process, alternating between adding a thin layer of egg mixture, cooking, and rolling until you have used all the egg mixture. Aim for about 4 to 6 layers, depending on your preference.

1. Adjust the shape of the Tamagoyaki by gently pressing the omelette together with your utensil as you roll each layer. This helps create a square shape and ensures a uniform appearance.

1. Once the Tamagoyaki is fully cooked, transfer it to a cutting board or plate. Allow it to cool slightly before slicing. Cooling helps the layers hold their shape.

1. Using a sharp knife, slice the Tamagoyaki into bite-sized pieces. Aim for clean, even cuts to showcase the layers within. Arrange the slices on a serving plate and garnish as desired.

The classic Tamagoyaki can be enjoyed warm or at room temperature. Its savory and slightly sweet flavors make it a versatile dish that can be enjoyed as a side dish, in a bento box, or as part of a larger meal.

Now that you've mastered the classic Tamagoyaki recipe, you can explore various flavor variations and creative twists in the upcoming chapters. Get ready to unleash your culinary creativity and elevate your Tamagoyaki game!

Chapter 5: Sweet Tamagoyaki Variations

While the classic savory Tamagoyaki is a delightful treat, there's a whole world of sweet variations waiting to be explored. In this chapter, we'll introduce you to some mouthwatering sweet Tamagoyaki recipes that are perfect for those with a sweet tooth. Get ready to indulge in these delectable creations!

Honey-Soy Tamagoyaki:
Ingredients:

- 4 large eggs
- 1 tablespoon dashi
- 1 tablespoon soy sauce
- 1 tablespoon honey
- 1/4 teaspoon salt
- Cooking oil or cooking spray for greasing the pan

Instructions:

Follow the same steps as the classic Tamagoyaki recipe (Chapter 4), replacing mirin with honey. The honey adds a subtle sweetness and enhances the overall flavor profile of the omelette. Adjust the sweetness to your preference by adding more or less honey.

Sweet Soy Glazed Tamagoyaki:
Ingredients:

- 4 large eggs
- 1 tablespoon dashi
- 2 tablespoons soy sauce
- 1 tablespoon mirin
- 1 tablespoon sugar

- 1/4 teaspoon salt
- Cooking oil or cooking spray for greasing the pan

Instructions:

Follow the same steps as the classic Tamagoyaki recipe (Chapter 4), but modify the seasoning. In a separate bowl, mix together soy sauce, mirin, sugar, and salt until the sugar is dissolved. Use this sweet soy glaze as the seasoning for each layer of the Tamagoyaki. The glaze adds a glossy finish and a delightful sweetness to each bite.

Matcha Tamagoyaki:

Ingredients:

- 4 large eggs
- 1 tablespoon dashi
- 1 tablespoon sugar
- 1 teaspoon matcha powder
- 1/4 teaspoon salt
- Cooking oil or cooking spray for greasing the pan

Instructions:

Follow the same steps as the classic Tamagoyaki recipe (Chapter 4), but incorporate matcha powder into the egg mixture. In a separate bowl, whisk matcha powder with sugar until well combined. Add the matcha-sugar mixture, along with the dashi and salt, to the beaten eggs. Whisk until all the ingredients are fully incorporated. The matcha adds a beautiful green hue and a subtle earthy flavor to the Tamagoyaki.

Vanilla-Cinnamon Tamagoyaki:
Ingredients:

- 4 large eggs
- 1 tablespoon dashi
- 1 tablespoon sugar
- 1 teaspoon vanilla extract
- 1/4 teaspoon ground cinnamon
- Cooking oil or cooking spray for greasing the pan

Instructions:

Follow the same steps as the classic Tamagoyaki recipe (Chapter 4), but infuse the egg mixture with the warm and comforting flavors of vanilla and cinnamon. In a separate bowl, mix together sugar, vanilla extract, and ground cinnamon until well combined. Add this mixture, along with the dashi, to the beaten eggs. Whisk until all the ingredients are fully incorporated. The vanilla and cinnamon create a delightful aromatic twist to the sweet Tamagoyaki.

Feel free to experiment with these sweet Tamagoyaki variations, adjusting the flavors and sweetness to suit your taste. These delicious creations can be enjoyed as dessert, a sweet snack, or even as a unique addition to your breakfast menu. Get creative and explore the world of sweet Tamagoyaki to satisfy your cravings and surprise your taste buds!

Chapter 6: Savory Tamagoyaki Variations

While the classic Tamagoyaki is a culinary delight on its own, there's a wide array of savory variations that take this dish to new heights. In this chapter, we'll introduce you to some tantalizing savory Tamagoyaki recipes that will satisfy your savory cravings and add exciting flavors to your table.

Vegetable Medley Tamagoyaki:
Ingredients:

- 4 large eggs
- 1 tablespoon dashi
- 1 tablespoon soy sauce
- 1/4 teaspoon salt
- 1/4 cup diced mixed vegetables (such as carrots, bell peppers, and mushrooms)
- Cooking oil or cooking spray for greasing the pan

Instructions:

Follow the same steps as the classic Tamagoyaki recipe (Chapter 4), but add a delightful vegetable medley to the layers. Saute the diced mixed vegetables in a pan with a little oil until slightly tender. Allow them to cool before incorporating them into each layer of the Tamagoyaki. The combination of savory eggs and colorful vegetables creates a nutritious and flavorful variation.

Cheese and Herb Tamagoyaki:
Ingredients:

- 4 large eggs
- 1 tablespoon dashi

- 1 tablespoon soy sauce
- 1/4 teaspoon salt
- 1/4 cup grated cheese (such as cheddar or mozzarella)
- 1 tablespoon chopped fresh herbs (such as parsley or chives)
- Cooking oil or cooking spray for greasing the pan

Instructions:

Follow the same steps as the classic Tamagoyaki recipe (Chapter 4), but incorporate the irresistible combination of cheese and herbs into the layers. Sprinkle grated cheese and chopped fresh herbs over each layer of the Tamagoyaki as you roll it. The melted cheese and fragrant herbs infuse the omelette with a burst of savory goodness.

Teriyaki Chicken Tamagoyaki:
Ingredients:

- 4 large eggs
- 1 tablespoon dashi
- 1 tablespoon soy sauce
- 1 tablespoon mirin
- 1/4 teaspoon salt
- 1/2 cup cooked and shredded teriyaki chicken
- Cooking oil or cooking spray for greasing the pan

Instructions:

Follow the same steps as the classic Tamagoyaki recipe (Chapter 4), but enhance the layers with the savory flavor of teriyaki chicken. Mix the shredded teriyaki chicken with a small amount of teriyaki sauce. Spread a thin layer of the chicken mixture over each layer of the Tamagoyaki as you roll it. The combination of juicy chicken and sweet-savory teriyaki sauce creates a mouthwatering Tamagoyaki experience.

Seafood Delight Tamagoyaki:
Ingredients:

- 4 large eggs
- 1 tablespoon dashi
- 1 tablespoon soy sauce
- 1/4 teaspoon salt
- 1/4 cup cooked and chopped seafood (such as shrimp, crab, or salmon)
- Cooking oil or cooking spray for greasing the pan

Instructions:

Follow the same steps as the classic Tamagoyaki recipe (Chapter 4), but elevate the flavors with a medley of seafood. Incorporate the cooked and chopped seafood into each layer of the Tamagoyaki as you roll it. The addition of succulent seafood lends a delightful briny flavor and a touch of luxury to the omelette.

Feel free to customize these savory Tamagoyaki variations to suit your preferences. Experiment with different vegetables, cheeses, meats, or seafood to create your own unique flavor combinations. These savory Tamagoyaki variations can be enjoyed as a main dish, in a bento box, or as a delightful addition to your dinner spread. Let your culinary creativity shine and indulge in the savory delights of Tamagoyaki!

Chapter 7: Tamagoyaki Sushi Rolls

Combining the flavors of Tamagoyaki with the artistry of sushi rolls creates a delightful fusion of Japanese culinary traditions. In this chapter, we'll explore the world of Tamagoyaki sushi rolls, where the delicate layers of the omelette meet the freshness of sushi ingredients. Get ready to roll up your sleeves and embark on a sushi-making adventure!

Ingredients:

4 large eggs

1 tablespoon dashi

1 tablespoon soy sauce

1/4 teaspoon salt

Nori sheets (seaweed sheets)

Sushi rice (cooked sushi rice seasoned with vinegar, sugar, and salt)

Assorted sushi fillings (such as cucumber, avocado, crab stick, and pickled vegetables)

Soy sauce, wasabi, and pickled ginger for serving.

Instructions:

1. Prepare the Tamagoyaki: Follow the basic Tamagoyaki technique (Chapter 3) to create a classic Tamagoyaki omelette. Let it cool slightly before slicing into thin rectangular strips. Set aside.

1. Prepare the Sushi Rice: Cook sushi rice according to the package instructions and season it with vinegar, sugar, and salt. Let the rice cool to room temperature before using.

1. Roll the Sushi: Place a sheet of nori on a sushi mat or a clean, damp kitchen towel. Moisten your hands with water to prevent the rice from sticking. Spread a thin, even layer of sushi rice over the nori, leaving a small border at the top edge.

1. Arrange the Fillings: Place a few strips of Tamagoyaki and your choice of assorted sushi fillings (such as cucumber, avocado, crab stick, or pickled vegetables) in a line across the center of the rice-covered nori sheet.

1. Roll the Sushi: Using the sushi mat or towel as a guide, start rolling the sushi tightly, applying gentle pressure to ensure a compact and secure roll. Wetting the top border of the nori will help seal the roll.

1. Slice and Serve: Once the sushi roll is tightly rolled, use a sharp knife to slice it into bite-sized pieces. Dip the knife in water before each slice for cleaner cuts. Arrange the sushi rolls on a platter and serve with soy sauce, wasabi, and pickled ginger for dipping.

1. Explore Variations: Don't be afraid to get creative with your Tamagoyaki sushi rolls. Experiment with different fillings, such as raw or cooked fish, tempura, or even other types of omelette. Play with sauces, toppings, and garnishes to create your own unique sushi roll creations.

Tamagoyaki sushi rolls make for an impressive and delicious addition to your sushi repertoire. The combination of the silky Tamagoyaki, fresh fillings, and seasoned rice offers a delightful harmony of flavors and textures. Enjoy these rolls as a tasty snack, part of a sushi platter, or even as a centerpiece at your next sushi-themed gathering.

Now that you've mastered Tamagoyaki sushi rolls, continue to expand your sushi-making skills with the exciting recipes and techniques we'll explore in the upcoming chapters. Get ready to unleash your creativity and roll your way to sushi perfection!

Chapter 8: Tamagoyaki Bento Box Ideas

Tamagoyaki is a versatile and delicious addition to any bento box, offering a protein-packed and visually appealing component to your meal. In this chapter, we'll provide you with creative Tamagoyaki bento box ideas that incorporate a variety of complementary ingredients. Get ready to pack your bento box with nutritious and satisfying delights!

Classic Tamagoyaki Bento:

1. Slice Tamagoyaki into rectangular pieces and place them in one compartment of your bento box.
2. Fill another compartment with steamed Japanese rice seasoned with furikake (Japanese rice seasoning) or sesame seeds.
3. Add a side of blanched or steamed vegetables, such as broccoli, carrots, or snap peas.
4. Include a small container of soy sauce or tamari for dipping the Tamagoyaki and rice.
5. Add a refreshing touch with a side of cucumber slices or a small salad of mixed greens.
6. Tamagoyaki and Teriyaki Chicken Bento:
7. Slice Tamagoyaki into rectangular pieces and place them in one compartment.
8. Add cooked and sliced teriyaki chicken in another compartment.
9. Include a portion of sushi rice or steamed Japanese rice.
10. Fill another compartment with a mix of stir-fried vegetables, such as bell peppers, zucchini, and mushrooms, seasoned with a touch of soy sauce and sesame oil.
11. Garnish with sesame seeds and add a side of pickled vegetables for added tang and flavor.

Tamagoyaki and Tempura Bento:

1. Slice Tamagoyaki into rectangular pieces and place them in one compartment.
2. Include a selection of vegetable tempura, such as sweet potato, green beans, and eggplant, in another compartment.
3. Add a portion of sushi rice or steamed Japanese rice.
4. Fill another compartment with a side of tangy daikon and carrot salad dressed with a light sesame vinaigrette.
5. Add a small container of tempura dipping sauce, soy sauce, or ponzu for dipping the tempura and Tamagoyaki.
6. Tamagoyaki and Onigiri Bento:
7. Slice Tamagoyaki into rectangular pieces and place them in one compartment.
8. Prepare onigiri (rice balls) filled with your choice of savory fillings, such as seasoned tuna, umeboshi (pickled plum), or grilled salmon. Place the onigiri in another compartment.
9. Include a side of steamed edamame or seasoned seaweed salad for a burst of umami flavor.
10. Add a refreshing touch with sliced radishes or cherry tomatoes.
11. Pack a small container of soy sauce or furikake for seasoning the onigiri and Tamagoyaki.

These bento box ideas provide a balance of flavors, textures, and nutrients, making them perfect for a satisfying and well-rounded meal. Feel free to customize the ingredients and add your personal touch to make your Tamagoyaki bento box even more enjoyable.

Continue to explore the possibilities with Tamagoyaki in the upcoming chapters, where we'll delve into more delicious recipes and creative ways to incorporate this versatile dish into your culinary repertoire. Get ready to elevate your bento box game with the delightful flavors of Tamagoyaki!

Chapter 9: Tamagoyaki Sandwich Creations

Tamagoyaki can be the star ingredient in creating delicious and unique sandwich creations. In this chapter, we'll explore the world of Tamagoyaki sandwiches, where the layers of the omelette meet a variety of fillings and spreads. Get ready to elevate your sandwich game with the delectable flavors of Tamagoyaki!

Classic Tamagoyaki Breakfast Sandwich:

1. Slice Tamagoyaki into rectangular pieces.
2. Toast two slices of bread of your choice.
3. Spread mayonnaise or Japanese Kewpie mayo on one side of each slice.
4. Layer the Tamagoyaki slices onto one slice of bread.
5. Add crispy bacon, sliced avocado, and fresh lettuce for added texture and flavor.
6. Top with the second slice of bread, mayo-side down.
7. Cut the sandwich in half and enjoy a delightful breakfast treat.

Tamagoyaki and Teriyaki Chicken Wrap:

1. Slice Tamagoyaki into rectangular pieces.
2. Heat a tortilla or wrap of your choice.
3. Spread a layer of teriyaki sauce on the tortilla.
4. Layer the Tamagoyaki slices onto the tortilla.
5. Add slices of teriyaki chicken, shredded lettuce, and julienned carrots for crunch.
6. Drizzle with additional teriyaki sauce or a tangy dressing.
7. Wrap the tortilla tightly and slice it in half for a satisfying and flavorful wrap.

1. Tamagoyaki and Vegetable Sushi Sandwich:
2. Slice Tamagoyaki into rectangular pieces.
3. Spread a layer of sushi rice on two slices of bread.
4. Add a sheet of nori (seaweed) on one side of the bread for an authentic sushi touch.
5. Layer the Tamagoyaki slices onto the bread.
6. Add thinly sliced cucumber, avocado, and julienned carrots for a refreshing crunch.
7. Sprinkle with sesame seeds and a drizzle of soy sauce or a sushi-inspired dressing.
8. Place the second slice of bread on top, rice-side down.
9. Cut the sandwich into bite-sized pieces for a unique and portable sushi-inspired snack.

Tamagoyaki Club Sandwich:

1. Slice Tamagoyaki into rectangular pieces.
2. Toast three slices of bread of your choice.
3. Spread your favorite sandwich spread, such as mayo or mustard, on each slice.
4. Layer one slice of bread with Tamagoyaki slices.
5. Add slices of roasted turkey or chicken, crispy bacon, lettuce, tomato, and avocado.
6. Place the second slice of bread on top.
7. Add another layer of Tamagoyaki slices, followed by more turkey or chicken, bacon, lettuce, tomato, and avocado.
8. Top with the third slice of bread, spread-side down.
9. Secure the sandwich with toothpicks or cut it into quarters for a satisfying and hearty club sandwich.

Feel free to experiment with different bread types, spreads, fillings, and sauces to create your own unique Tamagoyaki sandwich creations.

Whether you prefer a classic breakfast sandwich, a sushi-inspired wrap, or a stacked club sandwich, the combination of Tamagoyaki with other delicious ingredients will elevate your sandwich experience to new heights.

In the upcoming chapters, we'll continue to explore the versatility of Tamagoyaki and discover more exciting recipes to satisfy your culinary cravings. Get ready to enjoy the delightful flavors of Tamagoyaki in a variety of culinary creations!

Chapter 10: Tamagoyaki in Ramen and Noodle Dishes

Tamagoyaki adds a delightful touch to ramen and noodle dishes, bringing its unique flavor and texture to the mix. In this chapter, we'll explore various ways to incorporate Tamagoyaki into these comforting and flavorful dishes. Get ready to enhance your ramen and noodle experience with the deliciousness of Tamagoyaki!

Tamagoyaki Ramen:
Ingredients:

- 4 large eggs
- 1 tablespoon dashi
- 1 tablespoon soy sauce
- 1/4 teaspoon salt
- Ramen noodles (cooked according to package instructions)
- Chicken, pork, or vegetable broth
- Sliced green onions, sliced mushrooms, and bean sprouts for garnish
- Sliced Tamagoyaki for topping

Instructions:

1. Prepare the Tamagoyaki using the basic Tamagoyaki technique (Chapter 3). Slice it into thin rectangular pieces.
2. Cook ramen noodles according to the package instructions. Drain and set aside.
3. Heat the chicken, pork, or vegetable broth in a pot over medium heat. Bring it to a simmer.
4. Add cooked ramen noodles to the simmering broth and let them heat through.
5. In a separate small pot, warm the sliced Tamagoyaki in the

broth for a minute or two.

6. Divide the ramen noodles and broth among serving bowls.

7. Top with sliced Tamagoyaki, sliced green onions, sliced mushrooms, and bean sprouts.

8. Serve hot and enjoy the comforting combination of Tamagoyaki and ramen noodles.

Tamagoyaki Yakisoba:
Ingredients:

- 4 large eggs
- 1 tablespoon dashi
- 1 tablespoon soy sauce
- 1/4 teaspoon salt
- Yakisoba noodles (cooked according to package instructions)
- Sliced cabbage, sliced carrots, and sliced onions
- Vegetable oil for stir-frying
- Yakisoba sauce (available in stores) or a mixture of soy sauce, Worcestershire sauce, and ketchup

Instructions:

1. Prepare the Tamagoyaki using the basic Tamagoyaki technique (Chapter 3). Slice it into thin rectangular pieces.
2. Cook the yakisoba noodles according to the package instructions. Drain and set aside.
3. Heat a large skillet or wok over medium heat. Add a little vegetable oil.
4. Stir-fry the sliced cabbage, sliced carrots, and sliced onions until they are slightly softened.
5. Add the cooked yakisoba noodles to the skillet or wok and stir-fry for a few more minutes.
6. Drizzle yakisoba sauce or the soy sauce, Worcestershire sauce, and ketchup mixture over the noodles and vegetables. Toss to coat evenly.
7. Place the stir-fried yakisoba on a serving plate and top with sliced Tamagoyaki.
8. Serve hot and savor the combination of Tamagoyaki and flavorful yakisoba noodles.

Tamagoyaki Udon:
Ingredients:

- 4 large eggs
- 1 tablespoon dashi
- 1 tablespoon soy sauce
- 1/4 teaspoon salt
- Udon noodles (cooked according to package instructions)
- Udon soup base or a combination of soy sauce, mirin, and dashi
- Sliced green onions and nori strips for garnish
- Sliced Tamagoyaki for topping

Instructions:

1. Prepare the Tamagoyaki using the basic Tamagoyaki technique (Chapter 3). Slice it into thin rectangular pieces.
2. Cook the udon noodles according to the package instructions. Drain and set aside.
3. Prepare the udon soup base or a combination of soy sauce, mirin, and dashi in a pot. Bring it to a simmer.
4. Add the cooked udon noodles to the simmering soup base and let them heat through.
5. Divide the udon noodles and broth among serving bowls.
6. Top with sliced Tamagoyaki, sliced green onions, and nori strips.
7. Serve hot and relish the harmony of Tamagoyaki and thick, chewy udon noodles.

Feel free to adjust the ingredients and seasonings to your taste preferences. The addition of Tamagoyaki brings an extra layer of flavor and texture to these already delicious ramen and noodle dishes. Enjoy the comforting and satisfying combination of Tamagoyaki and noodles in various forms!

In the upcoming chapters, we'll continue to explore the versatility of Tamagoyaki and discover more exciting recipes to satisfy your culinary cravings. Get ready to enjoy the delightful flavors of Tamagoyaki in a variety of dishes!

Chapter 11: Tamagoyaki in Fried Rice and Stir-Fries

Tamagoyaki adds a delightful twist to fried rice and stir-fries, infusing them with its unique flavor and adding a touch of elegance. In this chapter, we'll explore creative ways to incorporate Tamagoyaki into these flavorful dishes. Get ready to elevate your fried rice and stir-fry game with the deliciousness of Tamagoyaki!

Tamagoyaki Fried Rice:
Ingredients:

- 4 large eggs
- 1 tablespoon dashi
- 1 tablespoon soy sauce
- 1/4 teaspoon salt
- Cooked white or brown rice (preferably chilled or day-old rice)
- Diced vegetables (such as carrots, peas, bell peppers, and onions)
- Diced cooked meat or shrimp (optional)
- Vegetable oil for stir-frying
- Soy sauce and sesame oil for seasoning

Instructions:

1. Prepare the Tamagoyaki using the basic Tamagoyaki technique (Chapter 3). Slice it into thin rectangular pieces.
2. Heat a large skillet or wok over medium heat. Add a little vegetable oil.
3. Stir-fry the diced vegetables (and meat or shrimp, if using) until they are tender-crisp.

4. Push the vegetables to one side of the skillet or wok and pour the beaten egg mixture into the other side.
5. Cook the eggs, stirring gently, until they are softly scrambled.
6. Add the cooked rice to the skillet or wok and mix well with the vegetables and scrambled eggs.
7. Drizzle soy sauce and a few drops of sesame oil over the fried rice. Toss to coat evenly.
8. Add the sliced Tamagoyaki to the fried rice and gently stir to distribute.
9. Cook for a few more minutes, allowing the flavors to meld together.
10. Serve hot and enjoy the delicious combination of Tamagoyaki and savory fried rice.

Tamagoyaki and Vegetable Stir-Fry:
Ingredients:

- 4 large eggs
- 1 tablespoon dashi
- 1 tablespoon soy sauce
- 1/4 teaspoon salt
- Sliced Tamagoyaki (thin rectangular pieces)
- Assorted vegetables (such as broccoli, bell peppers, carrots, snap peas, and mushrooms), sliced or cut into bite-sized pieces
- Garlic and ginger, minced
- Vegetable oil for stir-frying
- Stir-fry sauce (such as a combination of soy sauce, oyster sauce, and sesame oil)

Instructions:

1. Prepare the Tamagoyaki using the basic Tamagoyaki technique (Chapter 3). Slice it into thin rectangular pieces.
2. Heat a large skillet or wok over medium heat. Add a little vegetable oil.
3. Stir-fry the minced garlic and ginger until fragrant.
4. Add the assorted vegetables to the skillet or wok and stir-fry until they are tender-crisp.
5. Push the vegetables to one side of the skillet or wok and pour the beaten egg mixture into the other side.
6. Cook the eggs, stirring gently, until they are softly scrambled.
7. Mix the scrambled eggs with the vegetables in the skillet or wok.
8. Drizzle the stir-fry sauce over the mixture and toss to coat evenly.
9. Add the sliced Tamagoyaki to the stir-fry and gently stir to distribute.

10. Cook for a few more minutes, allowing the flavors to meld together.
11. Serve hot and relish the combination of Tamagoyaki and vibrant stir-fried vegetables.

Feel free to customize these recipes by adding your favorite ingredients, such as diced ham, shrimp, or additional spices and seasonings. The addition of Tamagoyaki brings a unique flavor and visual appeal to these already delicious fried rice and stir-fry dishes.

In the upcoming chapters, we'll continue to explore the versatility of Tamagoyaki and discover more exciting recipes to satisfy your culinary cravings. Get ready to enjoy the delightful flavors of Tamagoyaki in a variety of dishes!

Chapter 12: Tamagoyaki for Breakfast and Brunch

Tamagoyaki is a perfect addition to breakfast and brunch, offering a protein-packed and flavorful start to your day. In this chapter, we'll explore delicious ways to incorporate Tamagoyaki into morning meals. Get ready to kick-start your day with the delightful flavors of Tamagoyaki!

Tamagoyaki Breakfast Sandwich:
Ingredients:

- 4 large eggs
- 1 tablespoon dashi
- 1 tablespoon soy sauce
- 1/4 teaspoon salt
- Sliced Tamagoyaki
- English muffins or bagels
- Sliced cheese (such as cheddar or Swiss)
- Sliced tomato and fresh spinach leaves
- Optional: cooked bacon or ham slices

Instructions:

1. Prepare the Tamagoyaki using the basic Tamagoyaki technique (Chapter 3). Slice it into thin rectangular pieces.
2. Toast the English muffins or bagels until lightly crisp.
3. Layer a slice of cheese on the bottom half of each muffin or bagel.
4. Add a few slices of Tamagoyaki on top of the cheese.
5. If desired, add cooked bacon or ham slices.

6. Top with sliced tomato and fresh spinach leaves.
7. Place the top half of the muffin or bagel over the fillings.
8. Enjoy a hearty and satisfying Tamagoyaki breakfast sandwich.

Tamagoyaki Benedict:
Ingredients:

- 4 large eggs
- 1 tablespoon dashi
- 1 tablespoon soy sauce
- 1/4 teaspoon salt
- Sliced Tamagoyaki
- English muffins, split and toasted
- Poached eggs
- Hollandaise sauce
- Chopped chives or parsley for garnish

Instructions:

1. Prepare the Tamagoyaki using the basic Tamagoyaki technique (Chapter 3). Slice it into thin rectangular pieces.
2. Toast the English muffin halves until lightly crisp.
3. Place a few slices of Tamagoyaki on each muffin half.
4. Top with a poached egg on each Tamagoyaki layer.
5. Drizzle Hollandaise sauce over the eggs.
6. Garnish with chopped chives or parsley.
7. Serve this delightful Tamagoyaki Benedict for a special breakfast or brunch treat.

Tamagoyaki Breakfast Bowl:
Ingredients:

- 4 large eggs
- 1 tablespoon dashi
- 1 tablespoon soy sauce
- 1/4 teaspoon salt
- Sliced Tamagoyaki
- Cooked white or brown rice
- Sautéed vegetables (such as bell peppers, onions, and spinach)
- Avocado slices and cherry tomatoes
- Optional: Crispy bacon or smoked salmon

Instructions:

1. Prepare the Tamagoyaki using the basic Tamagoyaki technique (Chapter 3). Slice it into thin rectangular pieces.
2. Arrange a bed of cooked rice in a bowl.
3. Top the rice with sliced Tamagoyaki and sautéed vegetables.
4. Add avocado slices and cherry tomatoes.
5. If desired, add crispy bacon or smoked salmon for additional flavor.
6. Enjoy a nourishing and flavorful Tamagoyaki breakfast bowl.

Feel free to customize these breakfast and brunch ideas with your favorite ingredients and flavors. Tamagoyaki adds a delicious and protein-rich component to these morning meals, providing a satisfying and flavorful start to your day.

In the upcoming chapters, we'll continue to explore the versatility of Tamagoyaki and discover more exciting recipes to satisfy your culinary cravings. Get ready to enjoy the delightful flavors of Tamagoyaki in a variety of dishes!

Chapter 13: Tamagoyaki for Appetizers and Small Bites

Tamagoyaki lends itself perfectly to appetizers and small bites, offering bite-sized delights that are packed with flavor. In this chapter, we'll explore creative ways to incorporate Tamagoyaki into appetizers and small bites that are perfect for parties, gatherings, or simply enjoying as a tasty snack. Get ready to savor the deliciousness of Tamagoyaki in these delectable bites!

Tamagoyaki Sushi Rolls:
  Ingredients:

- 4 large eggs
- 1 tablespoon dashi
- 1 tablespoon soy sauce
- 1/4 teaspoon salt
- Nori sheets (seaweed sheets)
- Sushi rice (cooked sushi rice seasoned with vinegar, sugar, and salt)
- Assorted sushi fillings (such as cucumber, avocado, crab stick, and pickled vegetables)

Instructions:

1. Prepare the Tamagoyaki using the basic Tamagoyaki technique (Chapter 3). Slice it into thin rectangular pieces.
2. Place a sheet of nori on a sushi mat or a clean, damp kitchen towel.
3. Moisten your hands with water to prevent the rice from sticking.
4. Spread a thin, even layer of sushi rice over the nori, leaving a small border at the top edge.
5. Add a few slices of Tamagoyaki and your choice of assorted sushi fillings in a line across the center of the rice-covered nori sheet.
6. Roll the sushi tightly, using the sushi mat or towel as a guide. Wetting the top border of the nori will help seal the roll.
7. Slice the sushi roll into bite-sized pieces and arrange them on a platter.
8. Serve the Tamagoyaki sushi rolls with soy sauce, wasabi, and pickled ginger for dipping.

Tamagoyaki Skewers:
Ingredients:

- 4 large eggs
- 1 tablespoon dashi
- 1 tablespoon soy sauce
- 1/4 teaspoon salt
- Sliced Tamagoyaki
- Cherry tomatoes
- Cubed cheese (such as cheddar or mozzarella)
- Bamboo skewers

Instructions:

1. Prepare the Tamagoyaki using the basic Tamagoyaki technique (Chapter 3). Slice it into thin rectangular pieces.
2. Assemble the skewers by threading a cherry tomato, a slice of Tamagoyaki, and a cube of cheese onto each bamboo skewer.
3. Repeat the process for the desired number of skewers.
4. Arrange the Tamagoyaki skewers on a serving platter.
5. These skewers can be served as is or grilled briefly for a warm and melty cheese experience.
6. Serve the Tamagoyaki skewers as a delightful appetizer or party snack.

Tamagoyaki Stuffed Mushrooms:
Ingredients:

- 4 large eggs
- 1 tablespoon dashi
- 1 tablespoon soy sauce
- 1/4 teaspoon salt
- Sliced Tamagoyaki
- Button mushrooms (stems removed)
- Cream cheese or goat cheese
- Fresh herbs for garnish (such as parsley or chives)

Instructions:

1. Prepare the Tamagoyaki using the basic Tamagoyaki technique (Chapter 3). Slice it into thin rectangular pieces.
2. Preheat the oven to a moderate temperature.
3. Stuff each button mushroom with a small slice of Tamagoyaki and a dollop of cream cheese or goat cheese.
4. Place the stuffed mushrooms on a baking sheet.
5. Bake the mushrooms in the preheated oven until the cheese is melted and the mushrooms are tender.
6. Remove from the oven and garnish with fresh herbs.
7. Serve the Tamagoyaki stuffed mushrooms as a flavorful and elegant appetizer.

Feel free to experiment with different fillings, sauces, and presentations to create your own unique Tamagoyaki appetizers and small bites. These bite-sized delights are sure to impress your guests and leave them wanting more.

In the upcoming chapters, we'll continue to explore the versatility of Tamagoyaki and discover more exciting recipes to satisfy your culinary cravings. Get ready to enjoy the delightful flavors of Tamagoyaki in a variety of dishes!

Chapter 14: Tamagoyaki for Lunch and Dinner

Tamagoyaki can be a delicious and versatile addition to lunch and dinner menus, bringing its unique flavors and textures to a variety of dishes. In this chapter, we'll explore creative ways to incorporate Tamagoyaki into satisfying meals for lunch and dinner. Get ready to savor the deliciousness of Tamagoyaki in these delightful dishes!

Tamagoyaki Donburi (Rice Bowl):
  Ingredients:

- 4 large eggs
- 1 tablespoon dashi
- 1 tablespoon soy sauce
- 1/4 teaspoon salt
- Sliced Tamagoyaki
- Cooked white or brown rice
- Sliced cucumbers and shredded carrots for garnish
- Optional: Cooked protein of your choice (such as grilled chicken, beef, or tofu)
- Optional: Soy sauce or teriyaki sauce for drizzling

Instructions:

1. Prepare the Tamagoyaki using the basic Tamagoyaki technique (Chapter 3). Slice it into thin rectangular pieces.
2. Arrange a bed of cooked rice in a bowl.
3. Top the rice with sliced Tamagoyaki and your choice of cooked protein.

4. Add sliced cucumbers and shredded carrots for a refreshing crunch.
5. Drizzle soy sauce or teriyaki sauce over the bowl, if desired.
6. Enjoy a wholesome and satisfying Tamagoyaki donburi as a delicious lunch or dinner option.

Tamagoyaki Stir-Fried Noodles:
Ingredients:

- 4 large eggs
- 1 tablespoon dashi
- 1 tablespoon soy sauce
- 1/4 teaspoon salt
- Sliced Tamagoyaki
- Stir-fry noodles (such as yakisoba, udon, or rice noodles), cooked according to package instructions
- Assorted vegetables (such as bell peppers, carrots, snap peas, and mushrooms), sliced or cut into bite-sized pieces
- Garlic and ginger, minced
- Vegetable oil for stir-frying
- Stir-fry sauce (such as a combination of soy sauce, oyster sauce, and sesame oil)

Instructions:

1. Prepare the Tamagoyaki using the basic Tamagoyaki technique (Chapter 3). Slice it into thin rectangular pieces.
2. Heat a large skillet or wok over medium heat. Add a little vegetable oil.
3. Stir-fry the minced garlic and ginger until fragrant.
4. Add the assorted vegetables to the skillet or wok and stir-fry until they are tender-crisp.
5. Push the vegetables to one side of the skillet or wok and pour the beaten egg mixture into the other side.
6. Cook the eggs, stirring gently, until they are softly scrambled.
7. Mix the scrambled eggs with the vegetables in the skillet or wok.
8. Add the cooked stir-fry noodles to the skillet or wok and toss to combine.

9. Drizzle stir-fry sauce over the noodles and vegetables. Toss to coat evenly.
10. Add the sliced Tamagoyaki to the stir-fried noodles and gently stir to distribute.
11. Cook for a few more minutes, allowing the flavors to meld together.
12. Serve the Tamagoyaki stir-fried noodles as a delicious and satisfying lunch or dinner option.

Tamagoyaki and Vegetable Stir-Fry:
Ingredients:

- 4 large eggs
- 1 tablespoon dashi
- 1 tablespoon soy sauce
- 1/4 teaspoon salt
- Sliced Tamagoyaki
- Assorted vegetables (such as broccoli, bell peppers, carrots, snap peas, and mushrooms), sliced or cut into bite-sized pieces
- Garlic and ginger, minced
- Vegetable oil for stir-frying
- Stir-fry sauce (such as a combination of soy sauce, oyster sauce, and sesame oil)

Instructions:

1. Prepare the Tamagoyaki using the basic Tamagoyaki technique (Chapter 3). Slice it into thin rectangular pieces.
2. Heat a large skillet or wok over medium heat. Add a little vegetable oil.
3. Stir-fry the minced garlic and ginger until fragrant.
4. Add the assorted vegetables to the skillet or wok and stir-fry until they are tender-crisp.
5. Push the vegetables to one side of the skillet or wok and pour the beaten egg mixture into the other side.
6. Cook the eggs, stirring gently, until they are softly scrambled.
7. Mix the scrambled eggs with the vegetables in the skillet or wok.
8. Drizzle stir-fry sauce over the mixture and toss to coat evenly.
9. Add the sliced Tamagoyaki to the stir-fry and gently stir to distribute.
10. Cook for a few more minutes, allowing the flavors to meld

together.

11. Serve the Tamagoyaki and vegetable stir-fry as a delicious and nutritious lunch or dinner option.

Feel free to customize these recipes by adding your preferred proteins, spices, and seasonings. Tamagoyaki brings a unique flavor and visual appeal to these lunch and dinner dishes, providing a satisfying and delicious experience.

In the upcoming chapters, we'll continue to explore the versatility of Tamagoyaki and discover more exciting recipes to satisfy your culinary cravings. Get ready to enjoy the delightful flavors of Tamagoyaki in a variety of dishes!

Chapter 15: Tamagoyaki as a Side Dish

Tamagoyaki makes a fantastic side dish, adding a burst of flavor and protein to complement your main courses. In this chapter, we'll explore different ways to serve Tamagoyaki as a side dish, perfect for accompanying a variety of meals. Get ready to elevate your dining experience with the delightful flavors of Tamagoyaki!

Tamagoyaki Salad:
Ingredients:

- 4 large eggs
- 1 tablespoon dashi
- 1 tablespoon soy sauce
- 1/4 teaspoon salt
- Sliced Tamagoyaki
- Mixed salad greens
- Assorted vegetables (such as cherry tomatoes, cucumber slices, and shredded carrots)
- Salad dressing of your choice

Instructions:

1. Prepare the Tamagoyaki using the basic Tamagoyaki technique (Chapter 3). Slice it into thin rectangular pieces.
2. Toss the mixed salad greens, assorted vegetables, and sliced Tamagoyaki together in a bowl.
3. Drizzle your favorite salad dressing over the salad and toss to coat evenly.
4. Serve the Tamagoyaki salad as a refreshing and nutritious side dish.

Tamagoyaki Gyoza (Dumplings):
Ingredients:

- 4 large eggs
- 1 tablespoon dashi
- 1 tablespoon soy sauce
- 1/4 teaspoon salt
- Sliced Tamagoyaki
- Gyoza wrappers
- Water for sealing the dumplings
- Vegetable oil for pan-frying
- Dipping sauce of your choice (such as soy sauce, vinegar, and chili oil)

Instructions:

1. Prepare the Tamagoyaki using the basic Tamagoyaki technique (Chapter 3). Slice it into thin rectangular pieces.
2. Take a gyoza wrapper and place a slice of Tamagoyaki in the center.
3. Moisten the edges of the wrapper with water.
4. Fold the wrapper in half, sealing the edges and creating a crescent shape.
5. Repeat the process for the desired number of gyoza dumplings.
6. Heat a skillet with a little vegetable oil over medium heat.
7. Place the gyoza dumplings in the skillet, flat side down.
8. Cook until the bottoms are golden brown.
9. Add water to the skillet, cover, and steam the dumplings for a few minutes until the wrappers are cooked through.
10. Remove the lid and continue cooking until the water evaporates and the bottoms become crispy again.
11. Serve the Tamagoyaki gyoza dumplings with your favorite dipping sauce as a delicious and flavorful side dish.

Tamagoyaki Tempura:
Ingredients:

- 4 large eggs
- 1 tablespoon dashi
- 1 tablespoon soy sauce
- 1/4 teaspoon salt
- Sliced Tamagoyaki
- Tempura batter (available in stores) or homemade tempura batter
- Assorted vegetables (such as sweet potato, bell pepper, zucchini, and eggplant), sliced
- Vegetable oil for deep-frying
- Tempura dipping sauce

Instructions:

1. Prepare the Tamagoyaki using the basic Tamagoyaki technique (Chapter 3). Slice it into thin rectangular pieces.
2. Dip the sliced Tamagoyaki and assorted vegetables into the tempura batter, coating them evenly.
3. Heat vegetable oil in a deep fryer or a large pot to 350°F (180°C).
4. Carefully lower the battered Tamagoyaki and vegetables into the hot oil, frying them until golden brown and crispy.
5. Remove them from the oil and place them on a paper towel-lined plate to drain excess oil.
6. Serve the Tamagoyaki tempura alongside a dipping sauce of your choice as a delightful and crunchy side dish.

Feel free to experiment with different salad combinations, dumpling fillings, or tempura vegetables to suit your preferences. Tamagoyaki brings a unique flavor and texture to these side dishes, adding a touch of elegance to your dining experience.

In the upcoming chapters, we'll continue to explore the versatility of Tamagoyaki and discover more exciting recipes to satisfy your culinary cravings. Get ready to enjoy the delightful flavors of Tamagoyaki in a variety of dishes!

Chapter 16: Tamagoyaki for Special Occasions

Tamagoyaki can be the star of the show during special occasions, adding an elegant and flavorful touch to your celebratory meals. In this chapter, we'll explore exquisite ways to showcase Tamagoyaki for those memorable events. Get ready to impress your guests with the delightful flavors of Tamagoyaki on special occasions!

Tamagoyaki Sushi Platter:
Ingredients:

- 4 large eggs
- 1 tablespoon dashi
- 1 tablespoon soy sauce
- 1/4 teaspoon salt
- Sliced Tamagoyaki
- Sushi rice (cooked sushi rice seasoned with vinegar, sugar, and salt)
- Assorted sushi fillings (such as sashimi-grade fish, shrimp, crab, and vegetables)
- Nori sheets (seaweed sheets)
- Pickled ginger, wasabi, and soy sauce for serving

Instructions:

1. Prepare the Tamagoyaki using the basic Tamagoyaki technique (Chapter 3). Slice it into thin rectangular pieces.
2. Lay a sheet of nori on a sushi mat or a clean, damp kitchen towel.

3. Moisten your hands with water to prevent the rice from sticking.
4. Spread a thin, even layer of sushi rice over the nori, leaving a small border at the top edge.
5. Arrange slices of Tamagoyaki and your choice of assorted sushi fillings in lines across the center of the rice-covered nori sheet.
6. Roll the sushi tightly, using the sushi mat or towel as a guide. Wetting the top border of the nori will help seal the roll.
7. Repeat the process with different fillings and combinations to create a variety of sushi rolls.
8. Slice the sushi rolls into bite-sized pieces and arrange them on a platter.
9. Serve the Tamagoyaki sushi platter with pickled ginger, wasabi, and soy sauce for an impressive and delicious spread.

Tamagoyaki and Seafood Paella:

Ingredients:

- 4 large eggs
- 1 tablespoon dashi
- 1 tablespoon soy sauce
- 1/4 teaspoon salt
- Sliced Tamagoyaki
- Arborio rice or paella rice
- Assorted seafood (such as shrimp, mussels, clams, and squid)
- Onion, bell peppers, and peas
- Garlic and saffron threads for flavor
- Chicken or vegetable broth
- Olive oil for sautéing

Instructions:

1. Prepare the Tamagoyaki using the basic Tamagoyaki technique (Chapter 3). Slice it into thin rectangular pieces.
2. In a large paella pan or skillet, heat olive oil over medium heat.
3. Sauté the onion, bell peppers, and garlic until softened.
4. Add the rice and stir to coat it with the oil and vegetable mixture.
5. Pour in the chicken or vegetable broth, followed by the saffron threads for flavor and color.
6. Arrange the assorted seafood and sliced Tamagoyaki over the rice, pressing them gently into the mixture.
7. Cover the pan and let the paella cook over low heat until the rice is tender and the seafood is cooked through.
8. Once done, remove the pan from heat and let it rest for a few minutes before serving.
9. Serve the Tamagoyaki and seafood paella as a stunning and flavorful centerpiece for your special occasion.

Tamagoyaki Cheesecake:
Ingredients:

- 6 large eggs, separated
- 1/4 cup granulated sugar
- 1/4 teaspoon cream of tartar
- 8 ounces cream cheese, softened
- 1/4 cup milk
- 1/4 cup all-purpose flour
- 1 teaspoon vanilla extract
- Sliced Tamagoyaki for garnish

Instructions:

1. Prepare the Tamagoyaki using the basic Tamagoyaki technique (Chapter 3). Slice it into thin rectangular pieces.
2. Preheat the oven to 325°F (165°C).
3. In a mixing bowl, beat the egg yolks and sugar until light and fluffy.
4. In a separate bowl, beat the egg whites and cream of tartar until stiff peaks form.
5. In another bowl, mix the softened cream cheese, milk, flour, and vanilla extract until smooth.
6. Gradually fold the cream cheese mixture into the egg yolk mixture.
7. Gently fold in the beaten egg whites until well combined.
8. Pour the batter into a greased baking dish or springform pan.
9. Arrange the sliced Tamagoyaki on top of the batter as a decorative garnish.
10. Bake in the preheated oven for about 40-45 minutes, or until the cheesecake is set and lightly golden on top.
11. Allow the cheesecake to cool completely before refrigerating for a few hours or overnight.

12. Serve the Tamagoyaki cheesecake as a unique and delightful dessert for your special occasion.

Feel free to adapt these recipes to suit your taste preferences and the nature of your special occasion. Tamagoyaki brings an elegant and flavorful touch to these celebratory dishes, making them truly memorable.

In the upcoming chapters, we'll continue to explore the versatility of Tamagoyaki and discover more exciting recipes to satisfy your culinary cravings. Get ready to enjoy the delightful flavors of Tamagoyaki in a variety of dishes!

Chapter 17: Tamagoyaki with International Flair

Tamagoyaki's versatility allows it to seamlessly blend with international flavors, bringing a delightful twist to dishes from around the world. In this chapter, we'll explore how Tamagoyaki can be incorporated into various cuisines, adding an exotic touch to your culinary repertoire. Get ready to embark on a global culinary adventure with the international flair of Tamagoyaki!

Tamagoyaki Tacos:
  Ingredients:

- 4 large eggs
- 1 tablespoon dashi
- 1 tablespoon soy sauce
- 1/4 teaspoon salt
- Sliced Tamagoyaki
- Soft tortillas
- Grilled chicken or beef, sliced
- Sliced avocado, shredded lettuce, and diced tomatoes
- Sour cream or salsa for topping

Instructions:

1. Prepare the Tamagoyaki using the basic Tamagoyaki technique (Chapter 3). Slice it into thin rectangular pieces.
2. Warm the soft tortillas in a skillet or microwave.
3. Fill each tortilla with slices of Tamagoyaki, grilled chicken or beef, avocado, shredded lettuce, and diced tomatoes.
4. Top with sour cream or salsa, or your preferred taco toppings.

5. Serve the Tamagoyaki tacos as a fusion delight that combines the flavors of Japan and Mexico.

Tamagoyaki Fried Rice with Chinese Flavors:
Ingredients:

- 4 large eggs
- 1 tablespoon dashi
- 1 tablespoon soy sauce
- 1/4 teaspoon salt
- Sliced Tamagoyaki
- Cooked white or brown rice (preferably chilled or day-old rice)
- Diced vegetables (such as carrots, peas, bell peppers, and onions)
- Diced cooked chicken, shrimp, or ham (optional)
- Vegetable oil for stir-frying
- Soy sauce, oyster sauce, and sesame oil for seasoning

Instructions:

1. Prepare the Tamagoyaki using the basic Tamagoyaki technique (Chapter 3). Slice it into thin rectangular pieces.
2. Heat a large skillet or wok over medium heat. Add a little vegetable oil.
3. Stir-fry the diced vegetables (and meat or shrimp, if using) until they are tender-crisp.
4. Push the vegetables to one side of the skillet or wok and pour the beaten egg mixture into the other side.
5. Cook the eggs, stirring gently, until they are softly scrambled.
6. Add the cooked rice to the skillet or wok and mix well with the vegetables and scrambled eggs.
7. Drizzle soy sauce, oyster sauce, and a few drops of sesame oil over the fried rice. Toss to coat evenly.
8. Add the sliced Tamagoyaki to the fried rice and gently stir to distribute.
9. Cook for a few more minutes, allowing the flavors to meld

together.

10. Serve the Tamagoyaki fried rice with Chinese flavors as a fusion dish that marries the best of Japanese and Chinese cuisines.

Tamagoyaki Caprese Skewers:
Ingredients:

- 4 large eggs
- 1 tablespoon dashi
- 1 tablespoon soy sauce
- 1/4 teaspoon salt
- Sliced Tamagoyaki
- Cherry tomatoes
- Fresh mozzarella balls
- Fresh basil leaves
- Balsamic glaze for drizzling

Instructions:

1. Prepare the Tamagoyaki using the basic Tamagoyaki technique (Chapter 3). Slice it into thin rectangular pieces.
2. Assemble the skewers by threading a cherry tomato, a slice of Tamagoyaki, a fresh mozzarella ball, and a basil leaf onto each skewer.
3. Repeat the process for the desired number of skewers.
4. Arrange the Tamagoyaki Caprese skewers on a serving platter.
5. Drizzle balsamic glaze over the skewers for a tangy touch.
6. Serve the Tamagoyaki Caprese skewers as an international twist on the classic Italian Caprese salad.

Feel free to explore other international cuisines and adapt Tamagoyaki to suit different flavors and dishes. Let your creativity guide you as you infuse Tamagoyaki with international flair, creating unique and delicious combinations.

In the upcoming chapters, we'll continue to explore the versatility of Tamagoyaki and discover more exciting recipes to satisfy your culinary cravings. Get ready to enjoy the delightful flavors of Tamagoyaki in a variety of dishes!

Chapter 18: Tamagoyaki for Vegetarians

Tamagoyaki can be a fantastic option for vegetarians, providing a protein-rich and flavorful addition to vegetarian meals. In this chapter, we'll explore vegetarian-friendly ways to enjoy Tamagoyaki, ensuring that everyone can savor its delightful flavors. Get ready to elevate your vegetarian dishes with the versatility of Tamagoyaki!

Vegetable Tamagoyaki:

Ingredients:

- 4 large eggs
- 1 tablespoon soy sauce
- 1/4 teaspoon salt
- Assorted vegetables (such as bell peppers, carrots, zucchini, mushrooms, and spinach), finely diced or sliced
- Vegetable oil for cooking

Instructions:

1. In a bowl, beat the eggs and whisk in the soy sauce and salt until well combined.
2. Heat a non-stick skillet or Tamagoyaki pan over medium heat and lightly coat it with vegetable oil.
3. Pour a thin layer of the egg mixture into the skillet, swirling it to cover the bottom evenly.
4. Place a small amount of the diced or sliced vegetables over the egg mixture.
5. Starting from one end, gently roll the egg mixture into a cylinder shape, pushing it to the other end of the skillet.
6. Push the rolled egg to one end of the skillet and oil the exposed part of the skillet.
7. Pour another thin layer of the egg mixture into the skillet, lifting

the rolled egg to allow the mixture to flow underneath.

8. Place more vegetables over the egg mixture and roll it up again.

9. Repeat the process until all the egg mixture and vegetables are used.

10. Cook the rolled Tamagoyaki until it is set and lightly browned on all sides.

11. Remove from heat and let it cool slightly before slicing into bite-sized pieces.

12. Serve the vegetable Tamagoyaki as a protein-rich and flavorful addition to your vegetarian meals.

Tamagoyaki Sushi with Vegetables:
Ingredients:

- 4 large eggs
- 1 tablespoon soy sauce
- 1/4 teaspoon salt
- Sliced Tamagoyaki
- Sushi rice (cooked sushi rice seasoned with vinegar, sugar, and salt)
- Assorted vegetables (such as cucumber, avocado, bell peppers, and pickled vegetables)
- Nori sheets (seaweed sheets)
- Soy sauce and wasabi for serving

Instructions:

1. Prepare the Tamagoyaki using the vegetable Tamagoyaki recipe mentioned above. Slice it into thin rectangular pieces.
2. Lay a sheet of nori on a sushi mat or a clean, damp kitchen towel.
3. Moisten your hands with water to prevent the rice from sticking.
4. Spread a thin, even layer of sushi rice over the nori, leaving a small border at the top edge.
5. Arrange slices of Tamagoyaki and your choice of assorted vegetables in lines across the center of the rice-covered nori sheet.
6. Roll the sushi tightly, using the sushi mat or towel as a guide. Wetting the top border of the nori will help seal the roll.
7. Slice the sushi roll into bite-sized pieces and serve with soy sauce and wasabi as a delightful vegetarian sushi option.

Tamagoyaki and Tofu Stir-Fry:
Ingredients:

- 4 large eggs
- 1 tablespoon soy sauce
- 1/4 teaspoon salt
- Sliced Tamagoyaki
- Firm tofu, cubed
- Assorted vegetables (such as bell peppers, broccoli, carrots, and snap peas), sliced or cut into bite-sized pieces
- Garlic and ginger, minced
- Vegetable oil for stir-frying
- Stir-fry sauce (such as a combination of soy sauce, hoisin sauce, and sesame oil)

Instructions:

1. Prepare the Tamagoyaki using the vegetable Tamagoyaki recipe mentioned above. Slice it into thin rectangular pieces.
2. Heat a large skillet or wok over medium heat. Add a little vegetable oil.
3. Stir-fry the minced garlic and ginger until fragrant.
4. Add the cubed tofu and cook until lightly golden.
5. Add the assorted vegetables and stir-fry until they are tender-crisp.
6. Push the vegetables and tofu to one side of the skillet or wok and pour the beaten egg mixture into the other side.
7. Cook the eggs, stirring gently, until they are softly scrambled.
8. Mix the scrambled eggs with the vegetables and tofu in the skillet or wok.
9. Drizzle stir-fry sauce over the mixture and toss to coat evenly.
10. Add the sliced Tamagoyaki to the stir-fry and gently stir to distribute.

11. Cook for a few more minutes, allowing the flavors to meld together.
12. Serve the Tamagoyaki and tofu stir-fry as a satisfying and protein-rich vegetarian option.

Feel free to adapt these recipes to include your favorite vegetarian ingredients and flavors. Tamagoyaki offers a versatile and delicious addition to vegetarian meals, ensuring that everyone can enjoy its delightful flavors.

In the upcoming chapters, we'll continue to explore the versatility of Tamagoyaki and discover more exciting recipes to satisfy your culinary cravings. Get ready to enjoy the delightful flavors of Tamagoyaki in a variety of dishes!

Chapter 19: Tamagoyaki for Kids

Tamagoyaki can be a fun and delicious option for kids, introducing them to new flavors and textures while providing a nutritious meal. In this chapter, we'll explore kid-friendly ways to enjoy Tamagoyaki, making mealtime exciting and enjoyable for your little ones. Get ready to bring smiles to their faces with the delightful flavors of Tamagoyaki!

Tamagoyaki Bento Box:

Ingredients:

- 4 large eggs
- 1 tablespoon soy sauce
- 1/4 teaspoon salt
- Sliced Tamagoyaki
- Cooked rice
- Assorted bite-sized fruits and vegetables (such as grapes, cherry tomatoes, carrot sticks, and cucumber slices)
- Mini sandwiches or onigiri (rice balls) for variety
- Optional: Small cookie cutters for shaping rice or Tamagoyaki slices

Instructions:

1. Prepare the Tamagoyaki using the basic Tamagoyaki technique (Chapter 3). Slice it into thin rectangular pieces.
2. Arrange the sliced Tamagoyaki in the bento box, creating a colorful and eye-catching arrangement.
3. Fill small compartments of the bento box with cooked rice and shape them using small cookie cutters for added fun.
4. Add bite-sized fruits and vegetables to the remaining compartments.
5. Include mini sandwiches or onigiri for added variety.

6. Encourage your kids to mix and match the different components for a playful and enjoyable mealtime experience.

Tamagoyaki Pizza Roll-Ups:
Ingredients:

- 4 large eggs
- 1 tablespoon soy sauce
- 1/4 teaspoon salt
- Sliced Tamagoyaki
- Pizza sauce
- Shredded mozzarella cheese
- Assorted pizza toppings (such as diced bell peppers, mushrooms, and olives)
- Flour tortillas or whole wheat wraps

Instructions:

1. Prepare the Tamagoyaki using the basic Tamagoyaki technique (Chapter 3). Slice it into thin rectangular pieces.
2. Lay a tortilla or wrap flat on a clean surface.
3. Spread a thin layer of pizza sauce over the tortilla, leaving a small border at the edges.
4. Arrange slices of Tamagoyaki, shredded mozzarella cheese, and your choice of pizza toppings over the sauce.
5. Starting from one end, tightly roll up the tortilla, enclosing the fillings.
6. Slice the rolled tortilla into bite-sized pieces, securing each piece with a toothpick if needed.
7. Serve the Tamagoyaki pizza roll-ups as a delicious and kid-friendly twist on traditional pizza.

Tamagoyaki Pancakes:
Ingredients:

- 4 large eggs
- 1 tablespoon soy sauce
- 1/4 teaspoon salt
- Sliced Tamagoyaki
- Pancake mix (follow the instructions on the package)
- Optional: Chocolate chips, blueberries, or other pancake mix-ins

Instructions:

1. Prepare the Tamagoyaki using the basic Tamagoyaki technique (Chapter 3). Slice it into thin rectangular pieces.
2. Prepare the pancake batter according to the instructions on the package.
3. Heat a griddle or non-stick skillet over medium heat and lightly grease it.
4. Pour the pancake batter onto the griddle to form small circles.
5. Place a slice of Tamagoyaki on top of each pancake.
6. Optional: Add chocolate chips, blueberries, or other mix-ins to the pancakes.
7. Cook the pancakes until bubbles form on the surface, then flip them and cook until golden brown.
8. Serve the Tamagoyaki pancakes as a delightful and playful breakfast or brunch option.

Encourage your kids to get creative with their Tamagoyaki creations. Let them experiment with different shapes, colors, and combinations to make mealtime an enjoyable and interactive experience.

In the upcoming chapters, we'll continue to explore the versatility of Tamagoyaki and discover more exciting recipes to satisfy your culinary cravings. Get ready to enjoy the delightful flavors of Tamagoyaki in a variety of dishes!

Chapter 20: Creative Tamagoyaki Desserts

Tamagoyaki doesn't have to be limited to savory dishes. Its unique texture and sweet potential make it a versatile ingredient for creating delightful desserts. In this chapter, we'll explore creative ways to incorporate Tamagoyaki into desserts that will satisfy your sweet tooth. Get ready to indulge in the sweet and delicious flavors of Tamagoyaki!

Tamagoyaki French Toast:
   Ingredients:

- 4 large eggs
- 1 tablespoon milk
- 1 tablespoon granulated sugar
- Sliced Tamagoyaki
- Bread slices
- Butter for cooking
- Maple syrup, fresh fruits, or powdered sugar for serving

Instructions:

1. In a shallow bowl, whisk together the eggs, milk, and sugar until well combined.
2. Dip a slice of bread into the egg mixture, coating it evenly on both sides.
3. Place a slice of Tamagoyaki on one side of the bread and sandwich it with another bread slice.
4. Heat a skillet or griddle over medium heat and melt some butter.
5. Cook the Tamagoyaki French toast on the skillet until golden

brown on both sides.

6. Repeat the process for the remaining bread slices.

7. Serve the Tamagoyaki French toast with maple syrup, fresh fruits, or a dusting of powdered sugar for a delicious breakfast or dessert treat.

Tamagoyaki Ice Cream Rolls:
Ingredients:

- 4 large eggs
- 1 tablespoon milk
- 1 tablespoon granulated sugar
- Sliced Tamagoyaki
- Ice cream of your choice
- Toppings (such as crushed cookies, chocolate sauce, or fresh berries)

Instructions:

1. In a bowl, whisk together the eggs, milk, and sugar until well combined.
2. Heat a non-stick skillet or Tamagoyaki pan over medium heat and lightly coat it with oil.
3. Pour a thin layer of the egg mixture into the skillet, swirling it to cover the bottom evenly.
4. Cook the Tamagoyaki until it is set and lightly browned on both sides.
5. Remove the Tamagoyaki from the skillet and let it cool.
6. Cut the Tamagoyaki into thin strips or squares.
7. Take a sheet of plastic wrap and lay it flat on a clean surface.
8. Spread a layer of ice cream over the plastic wrap, then arrange the Tamagoyaki strips or squares on top.
9. Roll the ice cream and Tamagoyaki tightly in the plastic wrap to form a log shape.
10. Place the ice cream roll in the freezer for a couple of hours until firm.
11. Remove the plastic wrap and slice the ice cream roll into individual portions.
12. Serve the Tamagoyaki ice cream rolls with your favorite

toppings for a creative and delicious dessert experience.

Tamagoyaki Parfait:
Ingredients:

- 4 large eggs
- 1 tablespoon milk
- 1 tablespoon granulated sugar
- Sliced Tamagoyaki
- Vanilla or flavored yogurt
- Granola
- Assorted fresh fruits
- Honey or fruit syrup for drizzling

Instructions:

1. In a bowl, whisk together the eggs, milk, and sugar until well combined.
2. Heat a non-stick skillet or Tamagoyaki pan over medium heat and lightly coat it with oil.
3. Pour a thin layer of the egg mixture into the skillet, swirling it to cover the bottom evenly.
4. Cook the Tamagoyaki until it is set and lightly browned on both sides.
5. Remove the Tamagoyaki from the skillet and let it cool.
6. Cut the Tamagoyaki into small squares or strips.
7. In a glass or bowl, layer vanilla or flavored yogurt, Tamagoyaki squares, granola, and fresh fruits.
8. Repeat the layers until you reach the top of the glass or bowl.
9. Drizzle honey or fruit syrup over the parfait for added sweetness.
10. Serve the Tamagoyaki parfait as a delightful and colorful dessert option.

Feel free to let your imagination run wild with Tamagoyaki desserts. Experiment with different combinations, such as Tamagoyaki crepes, Tamagoyaki bread pudding, or Tamagoyaki-filled pastries. The possibilities are endless when it comes to creating sweet treats with Tamagoyaki.

With this, we conclude our Tamagoyaki Cookbook 101. We hope you've enjoyed the journey and discovered a variety of delicious ways to incorporate Tamagoyaki into your culinary repertoire. Happy cooking and savoring the delightful flavors of Tamagoyaki!

In this Tamagoyaki Cookbook 101, we embarked on a culinary journey exploring the versatility and deliciousness of Tamagoyaki. From its basic techniques to a wide range of recipes, we delved into the world of Tamagoyaki and discovered its ability to elevate meals in various ways. Whether you're a seasoned cook or a beginner in the kitchen, this cookbook provided you with the knowledge and inspiration to create delectable dishes centered around Tamagoyaki.

We began by introducing Tamagoyaki, its cultural significance, and its place in Japanese cuisine. We then explored essential equipment and ingredients needed to make Tamagoyaki successfully. With the basic Tamagoyaki technique in hand, we dove into a variety of recipes, including classic Tamagoyaki variations, sweet and savory options, and even international adaptations. We covered Tamagoyaki's role in breakfast, lunch, dinner, appetizers, and side dishes, showcasing its versatility in every meal.

We didn't forget about special occasions, offering you ideas on how to make Tamagoyaki shine during festive moments. We also catered to vegetarian diets, providing vegetarian-friendly Tamagoyaki recipes. For the little ones, we created kid-friendly Tamagoyaki dishes that are sure to please their taste buds. Finally, we explored the sweet side of Tamagoyaki, unveiling creative and delightful dessert options.

Throughout this cookbook, we emphasized the importance of experimenting and personalizing the recipes to suit your preferences. Tamagoyaki is a canvas for culinary creativity, allowing you to add your own unique touches and flavors.

We hope this Tamagoyaki Cookbook 101 has ignited your passion for cooking and inspired you to embark on a culinary adventure with Tamagoyaki. Whether you're cooking for yourself, your family, or entertaining guests, Tamagoyaki will bring joy and deliciousness to your table. So grab your spatula and let your imagination soar as you savor the delightful flavors of Tamagoyaki!

Happy cooking and bon appétit!